Dark Green

Emily Hunt

The Song Cave

Published by The Song Cave
www.the-song-cave.com
© 2015 Emily Hunt
Design and layout by Mary Austin Speaker

ISBN: 978-0-9884643-9-1
Library of Congress Control Number: 2015931471

FIRST EDITION

for Laura

To the faithful Absence is condensed presence.

EMILY DICKINSON

Table of Contents

FIGURE THE COLOR OF THE WAVE SHE WATCHED

goodbye gone kin like water
gone half, first self,
where is that friend
who happened to smoke
the first beautiful sky
where are the hours
she filled to see sink
those hollow shapes made
by wind, goodbye
cleared history, swept steps,
goodbye what's left
the weather, which leaves
slap and fret to explain
if only the weather
were how it was, the weather
has nothing to do, goodbye
lies I meant deeply
goodbye to each
flowering shock
ahead in the garden
the garden was paper
a plan
stabbed by trees and then
a stripped plot, goodbye
little war after war

a cold goodnight to
both ends of silence
did it begin, did I skate
past the omen, exquisite
caution my armor
I pretended to shed, dear
blank reply, radical portrait
hung on a cloud
girl with big shovel
inventing the flurry
oh lose me my snow

AMERICA

No one's around,
their respect for me has been receding
since my last vision where I was
on a ship and I could feel
the motion of the journey.
The frozen shards of rain
hit the sea so beautiful
the first slow hundred days.
I could see them through a little hole.
I tried to go to sleep
standing I imagined
going very far.
The fourth or fifth place might be
a kind of climbing over
the feeling of the group.
They didn't make the land
they just walked across it
rearranging, so I was there.

BEGINNER

And if the sky was round
and being filled
in November, the dark month appeared
smaller, and later
a kind of gray.
My arm was out the window.
Fall bled forward.
The upper edge of the whole sun
shifted something higher.
You were there, with me in the yards,
sometimes blue
in your clothes.
We spoke of the morbid.
Sparks seemed to spread from it.
Often a spawn of frogs
the impression of which
weakened as it lasted.
We appeared
to see nature, the sky
rose and all that should be green
appeared to us in autumn.
And these plain faces existed,
passing underneath.
In red light, we acted alone.
Two prisms, one upon the other.

Little kids played soccer
by the twisted corn.
The sun slid in the grooves.
The border spread
while we were eating dinner.

I WAS THE GIANT FACTORY

I went there every day

I did care about my job, its feeling wrong and endless,

the smooth machines, their heavy curves,

the rows of windows, revolving doors,

what filled the air, a thousand locks,

one looming cage, I'd only watch

Others there said little

and in the space they left

I slid invisibly, measuring, testing, slowing

what they saw in me and one of them

I decided I could hate

or love like I admired

HOLIDAY INN

It's hard to breathe at the mechanic
where the cars are midair

and the men are lying on the floor
out my window, examples of mountains

my car lived behind the house where the owner was dying
I didn't want to come to myself that way again

on the ceiling I drew something
to delete an end

it could describe black
and pass through text, like reading

on vacation, veering from a series
lying on the floor

a symptom of the universe
as common as the beach

*

climbing to the vending machine
is also not intimate

the bed is higher
to protect it

and nothing like the highway
the ferns are growing in space

the phone like a prop
is closest to the dragon fly

and bland lively gnats on the cracked ledge
where the air below the sky is

a sense and Virginia or
Paris Blue Street of Strength and small bug

fake wood and cracked dragon
chocolate and soap a feeling

I couldn't make a statement about
this beginning breaking like a broken cloud

something cold and what I am
and other cars, no food around

the bad hotel, no common air
in rain, expensive quiet

poured from the sun
I rest my soda by the stone

ORIGINAL

I copy myself
and release my replica
into an olive grove

She is real, just a second

We race to find little foods to fix her
She eats what I know and runs with it

Her pleasures babble in the grove, they tell me
I should be able

SYMBOLS

The one above me is solid, dark, and simple.
Below him there's a light
but between him and the light
a symbol of the light
so when I press
the symbol of him
nothing changes
and when I press the symbol of the light
I light up
the woman beside me
as someone here before
bent the light toward her.

WHIPPED BY NATURE

correct, sweet,
cruel whatever
fate we drag
night to the pond
and that same day
night falls –
who is who
who is heinous
whose dreams eat water

SAY IT IS SUMMER

he is minding his business
grilling a white gull
in its blue yard

FOR FLOWERS

how pretty
how exact is nothing
how booming and direct are the fields

and the flowers, fearless
stare happily out from a surface

how mine, that rubber heart
speeding, vicious, how known
is the sky, still here
and reaching for flowers of flowers

A CONVERSATION

I wish I could draw a picture to explain
I think it would be a circle
and you inside the circle
and me outside the circle
pointing to the ground, to my part of the sky
I would be wearing a shirt the color of pain inside the circle

the sun might be above us
touching everything
you could turn to me
to talk
and it might be easy in the picture

SUNDAY

My landlord is dying.
She lives in the room next to mine.
Sometimes I wake to her husband
asking her questions like
do you want to end it
you're wearing me out.
Only once I saw inside their place. It looked full.
The bed was near the door.
As we talked, I thought of their exchanges
passing in and out of my sleep.
This morning I waited a long time
for the cars from both sides
to finish their passing
and I crossed my street.
I sat down on a bench
in Luther A. Clark Memorial Chapel.
The chapel is a patch of grass
between the road and the locked cemetery.
The fence billows out where the steel is bent
by some kind of pressure built over time.
The bushes are carved flat
and they look weak near the ground
where their thin, peeling branches are exposed.
There is a ragged teal pine
alone near the center,

exhaust in the air.
A dark blue tarp
tied over a roof on the block,
another opened and black from a fire.
And there are buds on the tree
over this grave.
The day before she died was exceptionally sunny.
One could imagine a kind of law.
A bare sky and heat.
She sat on our porch
while I vacuumed.

ANOTHER TIME STOPPED

when I thought back on it
it was drenched on the road
lit up under red leaves
in front of its death
and dazed in the shower
this evening
bare under water
lit by the weak light I've intended
to replace time and time again
I realized I needed
once I stepped through the steam
to tell you something beautiful
before I went into
what had been true under water

ROUGH BELIEF

you were the daffodil
leaning over a history book
memorizing Pompeii
for a dead TV

REFLECTION NOT YET LINKED TO ANOTHER

on slick roads I see
dark streaks
through this particular
day as it rises
and I know this year I've done something
foolish
but know I won't know what
it was for another

LOVE IS A GOOD THING RUNNING

I found a good thing
I am sure of it
a small blue whirling pool in the wood floor of my living room
I step over it
a silver minnow on my pillow
I sleep next to it

twice with it
I painted my walls
and they change in wide light
like everything
it's hard
and I made it
it both belongs to
and reminds me of
itself

the problem is I hope
for a beginning running
in place of something astonishing
pointing with the hands of the wild
hidden person next to me
directly at that dot
I have pictured
and drawn in little pictures

on the little papers
I drop

and I hope everything
behind me was there in order
to push me toward this
and that, with slick eyes
I can navigate now
the shadows of these buildings springing
up by the dusty grooves
I'm making sprinting

the thing is the thing
is screwed
into the expanding wall
of someone else's will

my reflection bounces on its surface
as toward it I string myself
openly ridiculous
as light
and like a silver body in a murky pool
it turns when it sees me seeing it.

WHAT STUNNING PRIVILEGE

do you also know me

fake frenzy who wrote me

silk roses I bruised

toy arm I bent into sleep

a question erased

once it was memory

this chatting tin fate

the cold feathers it wears

erased the split tree

where I sat I belong

the very cracked sky

whose wet leaves

I grew in my sleep

those hours that open

a year I can touch

YOU MUST BE SO TIRED

I hope New York is beautiful
the streets in this weird sun
I wish I could be there sometimes
when you're there, it feels like you're working on a day with
    everyone at once
and at the end, before you go down into the subway tired
there's this communal relief in the dark
and then it's bright on the platform
and you can spend so long
just looking at people's clothes
imagining them as children
picturing them yelling or having sex in nice apartments
and if you get caught staring it doesn't matter
because it's really what the train becomes
a break from life to stare, say nothing about it
and move on
and if you're moody on the train a million people are moody
and their sweaty neck is near your hand
and you're holding onto the same metal rod
and you can be rude or particularly kind
and then it's gone
here, everyone's days feel more encased
and then, more observed
less like a thousand plain, frenzied lines
side by side

sometimes I do feel like one of those Russian eggs
split down the center in gold
sitting on a shelf, growing more complicated and garish
the longer you look
the longer I look
though I could say the same for then and now, generally, always,
then is broad, it moves quickly and we change it
now sits still and heavy and open and intricate
now I am eating cold green beans in a library cubicle and
    writing only to you
the window is black and I'm scared of my head
yesterday was a good day
I just didn't want to be seen
as far as all the other stuff goes
maybe it comes down
to time spent, the shared, the known
the escaping what was shared
that hurts

A FAVORITE STORY

I take him for walks
he pulls me through slush and the clouds barely move
an iron fence on my loop cuts off snow from more snow

THE CROSSING OVER

The crossing over is never for good
and always unsure.
But I do know this year has been lighter.
I've moved around it freely, apart from the day
I read too many emails from my past.
That morning I felt vast and nauseous
like the air at the center of four people
looking for a heart inside a ghost.
I moved through my house
doing the small things I had to
thinking of more sleep.
My friend picked me up
and we drove through an odd light.
Every corner, every street held
some dissolving feeling.
After a few miles we stopped
and walked to where the land met the river.
Her silver car was parked at the edge of the field
holding silence far from us.
I had never seen her cry before.
I talked for her, about our town, its theatre,
pathetic and charming,
and how each act tended to collapse
into some simple display:
five people, a chair, a door to the next world.

How to bring a new figure close
was like taking a globe, turning it once
and placing it back on its pedestal.
How huge this made one feel, and how empty.
She included me in her confusion
and I felt useful. I wanted to be like her
enough to understand myself
though I knew that even if I were
or even once I could, I'd be mixed up
in some older mystery.
She may be on another coast by then
or out at sea, taking notes.
I may have moved to where there is no snow.
We may barely be in touch.
Every now and then
there was the silent progress of a car
cutting through a farther field.
The sun was lower.
It reminded me of hell.
It felt like years had passed
and we were the only ones who knew.

SPRING

last night I suffocated
a gorgeous grasshopper

it was the fifteenth
I killed this May

PARADISE LOST

no more of talk
where god or angel guest
with man, as with his friend,
familiar us'd
to sit indulgent
and with him partake
rural repast,
permitting him the while
venial discourse unblam'd:
I now must change
those notes to tragic;
foul distrust, and breach
disloyal on the part of man
revolt, and disobedience:
on the part of heav'n
now alienated, distance and distaste,
anger and just rebuke,
and judgment giv'n,
that brought into this world
a world of woe,
sinne and her shadow death,
and miserie, deaths harbinger
sad task, yet argument
not less but more heroic then the wrauth

of stern Achilles on his foe pursu'd
thrice fugitive about Troy wall;
or rage

NO TITLE

a kid on a floating dock,
a weird extra facing the first,
there are four of them

the place is really floating made neatly of trees
one makes a joke on the ocean
the world rushes to enrich it
clouds float over their parents
the sky and the water are blue and the rest of the world
doesn't touch the beach

MOVIE

I sat in the safety of my age
all the blanks in front of it
flashed far enough away
I tried to love at least her
she was better than her beauty and she woke
face-down, arms astray, a wreck
haunted by what she had divulged
I saw I was inside
the brutal black lace of each tree the night held
I saw my character would always watch me

IT'S GOOD TO BE IN YOUR PAINTINGS

for example you're alone in me
though out here on my own
in my fixed legacy
I go to the gorge
on my way to one river
they tell me take your dog
out of the lake
and holding my animal
leashed to a tree
judging can be very subtle
Massachusetts is dark green

BUMPING INTO HER

she thought I was you
so I told her about us
and she asked how you were
as she slipped in her letter
I saw her last week from afar
and forgot whether
she knew for a minute
by the look on her face
it was clear she could tell
I looked down
we shook hands in the grass
she was confused, I explained
you had moved
but I was still living here

FOREST

I say what I believe
and a tree falls through me

MUSEUM

not a dangerous thing
there is rain below the floor
the course of history, a city
so close to what the world is like

14

she loops through the guide
the neighbors have hired her
she looks at their Ovaltine and the brown eyes of their children
the girl lifts her sweater, touching her spine
a player is injured,
his solid leg twists quickly, and again in the replay
walking down the same
hills she has biked
without hands or feet
through damp and blue trees
back to the scared
sleeping bloods of the people of her
she hears pipes letting water out onto the lawn

BLUE TAKES OVER

blue takes over
green gives us the lush
yellow lies down
violet is so godly
chartreuse kills me
white is a zero
another fleck in the corner
taupe lives in fear
lilac has no family
bronze dreads the morning
sapphire circles mars
crimson seldom appears
slate is an allegory
purple's just a theory
coral absorbs the animals
fuchsia pushes past us
manila is pathetic
rose wants maroon
it isn't easy being beige
twisting pure and dry
through everything good
puce lives underground
orange left the rainbow
mauve is lost again
and like blue gazes

black touches black
pink gets bored
cyan is cold
sinking in the sea
magenta changes lives
indigo takes forever
white keeps its distance
open in the sliding light
cerulean lives through blue
the world is drenched in lavender
speaking through the throat
extravagant and frantic
emerald is a heartbreaker
imagine you are gray
as it eats through
azure, indigo is warm
medium snow pretty
and alien in quality
platinum is lusty
and flits generously around
struck by sienna
cadmium is magnetic
jade is a winner
viridian is impressive
plum broods with mustard
burgundy is permanent
celadon can't take it anymore
pistachio wants to die today

sage has no shadow
in the trashcan of the bathroom by the bog
carmine was briefly happy
emerging in great leaves
silver grieves vividly
on roofs as dust
comes and goes
unchecked like a huge
sweeping joy and steel
is frozen as noises
ivory clenches
low, so feeble
sepia is alluring
charcoal is silent
gold has many allies
fluorescents found the shoreline
navy is permanent
gray is alive today
floating in the clouds
brown married green again
dark cornflower can't be explained

ARRIVAL

standing under the tree above it
I once froze two under an olive one
and called them, tangled, my parents

bones I may never see
walking past, I don't remember
predicting this

the sun was not red
I call it red now and it runs
I do not grow rapidly

toward the dense blank onto which
I have stumbled
I have slipped into trees, happened upon green, sun, and
toward nothing I list

SONG

what is the difference
between an empty square
and a square of light

one knows
and one knows
one's cold role in love

IN THE TRUNKS OF CERTAIN TREES, DELICATE PEOPLE

you are now faced with explaining
one commanding image

choirs are places in which to sing
because they are made of wood
angels are the strongest parts of cities
knots are towns, a town can be common
within the space of six short years
a form will appear
abused
art is a battle and attractive
art is finally a book
madonnas are not pretty women
their poses were tragic, very natural, they were painted
and this is impossible, broken glass
dedicated to memory, ugly
my failure is what makes his failure clear to me now
Kandinsky, his library, his love and him

WINTER

my blue light arrived
from Springfield today
to imitate the sun

RESEARCH

It's too dark to compare
I snatch back my hands
which had sunk just to see
anything different
and years they hang drying, wearing
these slipping black rings

I WAS VERY ANGRY

I paused to enjoy the view
I began again
I tore myself in half

the air was dropping
rain into a black hole
and God was scared too

he rolled the windows up

I screamed

no one for miles in the American painting turned a head

I held my sleeve I screamed again and felt no different in the
        dream a tiny rock
rolled down a crevice
also silt
felt like sand amassing

feels like I feel moving as I note
sweet grasses gently everywhere
the lack below my feet

as I enter yet another
McDonald's by the sea

I think about when it was gone
and night sat on this lot, stored its stars here breathing

I eat the salt, I plummet
into memory where I find
memory is sick of me
and I remember reality

AFTERNOON

this one is deep blue
drag the tube, the rug pulls back
the dusty body nudges and rolls
    suck up flea eggs under a paper sign
    suck up flea eggs under a stained light
let the house get big
pull it across
push it against the grain
along the grain
over the veins of cloth petals
opening under the dust
the attachment falls off and the sound continues
it sits on its side like the leg of dead time
this one is red with thick looping lines
fat seeds
tropical
flat story of work
get to the life in the tassels
the fine reeds of the rocker
the grooves in the phone
valleys of the wide mossy chair
cold on the smooth flecked tiles
lead the low end around
hit the hip
suck up more temporary air

move the vast table to the done room
lift one side and shift it
the other
life one side and shift it
the other
push it over the border
the chairs into each other
stand on the center of the naked dense one
can they cling to the socks
in the hair, cupboards
the tin bell on the sill
the pair of green dolphins
snaking around the globby dish
hide the bread, the two cups
lift the bagged clothes far away
in ribbony paths from the house
for the dripping trees
splat on the snowy garbage plastic
let the loads multiply
run water into the base of the bomb
a sip to the line
set it where the wood shows through the creamy paint
open the swollen drawers
let one fall
scan the room to see what it might reach
what places it could miss
squeeze through with the bags

come back
close the door, the doors, lock the last door
back the borrowed gray car over the poppies and weeds
the spotted shed feathers of birds
dark soil where the hose washed out the liquid the trash left

EVENING

worms pass through their lives
in slow, mindless lines
by shitting dirt they eat
I think of them in crowds
when something's rotting

COMPUTER

the music was blank when I found the news
and today was summer again,
the time people take things
they no longer want,
maybe never needed,
spread them out on tables, and sell them
as the shadows grow from under spring

how I'm here, is why I'm lost,
and who I love, I live across
from a hundred graves, birds float by
like cuts in the clouds, a man and his wife
dragged a girl to a tree
and hung her high enough to live
low enough to brush the ground

YOUR SPINNING WHEEL

on behalf of the object, on behalf of the ego
consider this spinning

a timeworn dream
it is no secret

nor anything new
wicked fool

do not stop wait
consider the fruit

the dry leaf sticks
do not approach touch

or move the tree
you won't want to go on if you do

2013

black ridges, like built shadows
where the lane lines were

dirt on the snow,
rain on the snow,
killers at school

the outdoors are the same
full of gorgeous product, mostly irreversible, and the sun
clashes with new clouds

the actors are made of wood in the meadow
even being in the world gets old
lying in the spring together on the phone

THE PLACE I SAT BESIDE

I didn't know I had chosen
the earth as it separates
on Wednesday, the strange place to cry

TOWN FAIR

my neighbors' heavy shoes
hang up into the night,
proof I ever was
my own, the stars around,
my venture out
into the hours,
I see the crowd I hear the crowd
not wicked it's young, to hold your hand

LAST TOOL ON EARTH

the riches he makes
in the holes of the sea

the thoughts it owes
to the makers of grand
structures that kill

the bloom in the window
like the leaves of a country
unknown to the mind

circling shark, dangerous heart

the money it needs

the love that it gives

paying away

magical light from the body

from the body true light

suspended like techno

the shadows of mattresses

in moon of the city

the makers of brick
pillar
road
bulb
cloud

what is loss worth
will it fly loosely

and break down

the leaves of a country
far-off enough
enough to be desolate
unfinished activity
closely attending
to the wheels of the bike
the sky its inside
a white painted earth

is it exactly
visual to survive

metal in blood
human alive

down in the cell
the money it is
the language it can't
take off the dream

TV

I have not been outdoors
tearing my junk mail in parts.
I read a letter that told me
my friends are important
because I'm not really
alone when I'm walking.
I think of her, how true
the thrill, there was something
you gave to me, I give it away.
Here by my working
a cold body in water
my fish sometimes pauses
in softness.
His fins are like hair.
He'll dart up
for a few specks of food
I drop from above
and I wonder how loud
his world might be.
Trembling at the top,
he'll suck back the air from a bubble
he made with his breath and then bolt
down and away, to return
to the same situation –
the pebbles, the plant,

which hovers so dumbly,
its roots loosened
from a rock that once squashed them,
a surface that wonders beyond him –
and pressing his self
against an edge, he'll nearly disappear,
distorted, a mark of nerves now he comes
to the curve nearest me.
He looks out, living and small, already I care.
Locking my door I laugh at the size of his heart.
I admit that I dread
the moment I find him.
I see it in flashes
stiff and impossible
by the bank in autumn or pain.
A hot planet is troubling
the darkness above
a Chilean desert
and again I'm awake.
The sky is a luxury
a slow outside, and then
I go there.
Some seconds long
I carry my TV
down to the bricks, the rocks and trucks in my yard I forget.
I don't know,
where white gravel pools by the car.
I am trashless now, I am not.

A cat in the woods
meets a cat in the snow.
My friend remembers the death.
Dense world I am finally leaving like air.
What's moving inside, a subject
who seems to be loving.
A movie is growing around him.

VIEW FROM A REGULAR FANTASY

love flies these planes
they are small and there's room for them
they make loops

for a while each mountain stands
small as the years
that matter

and the red loud lights
a dog in the drive

black lump is it love
can it walk
sweat like today
by the field, our own dull paint

still flies
by the scared square room, by the west each day
we should not be shocked
by ourselves

ENGLISH

A row of trees.
A crackhead asleep at the library.
Air conditioning.
The ill.
An equilateral triangle.
A woman barking.
A poster, a painting, liquid, bread.
A hand through a wall.
Another parabola.
Rain.
Regard all that occurs as
a few shallow stairs.
A horse lying in a forest.
A dark tale of the Western frontier.
A teenager in Ohio.
An unbelievable amount of bats, in streams of hundreds.
A second, secret vocation.
An arrow, surprising anyone.
A weapon / sleep
"what are we going to do with the rest of our lives"
"what is left of us"
A performing leopard
Curls of bark
The lamps
A famous man, a singer you feel for

A wet computer in a bag of rice

A candle a flame a face on a banner

A parking garage, a heavy round tree

The feathers on the breasts of certain parrots are strictly yellow

In ravens, only the exposed portion exhibits iridescence

A plastic bottle

A perfect piece of toast, he died

The cat returning through a hole in the bedroom screen, he did die

Groceries, dark metals and wine, he died collecting gold

The written world without an eye to move it, he's dead and such

A toaster sound / the phone his face is gone

He bought it with the cash he made raking leaves and filling
    black bags

Settled into an endless lush slope of ivy overlooking a parking
    lot, he's just dead

A black plastic suit, a coin in the dirt

You were in this town in the rain, but he's dead it's a city

What you said made me picture the earth, dying

A circle of women shifted to let in two men, one was dead I think

A room of velvet that collapses when you find it, there's a dead
    person in it

I went into the dark square and turned on the light

HD he's dead

New York he's crossing the water

He's carrying me

A train in the rain on the plain and all that scenery

Brain of the morning say you're frightened, not afraid

Nature, he crosses you, he's through

Thrill of the plain
deer and their mother

walking on a mirror
in the meadow unavoidable
showing against many hours
he had been more
it was like Lucy, John
a form on the wall
I can't imagine, Irene said
and she wasn't him

he died at me, unclassically

;

painted body inches over a blossoming elm

sewagey puddle

mosquito on bus cloth

ticket in the pocket

Civic, Galant, Hyundai, Accord

;

it was kind of one way for a while
for a long time it had been like that

;

no one could stop him
none of us
The thought of him occurs
it's a liberty
a slap in the face
A mark to the senses
Unsymmetrical, death verges on life
it's a liberty
it's passionate until it is silent
that's when it stops, enticingly
death throws itself at anything, in all of the words
he wasn't alive
A little glow worm, a little kid
Zazie in the metro, zombie on the light rail
walking along I pull a tree from the earth
no one sees me
(It's a feeling, like death)
Now it's lying in front of me
and the yellow lines of the crosswalk are lying under it

and the heavens are below
the twilight zone and all that
and all those people crossing made it fast to keep going
so I'm with them shopping
I turn my head underground and sense and see the concrete
    go by
there are holes in it where the air sits and then drifts, tinyish
It's like sand like that
But cold
they don't feel it, I feel death
motioning at my kidself
I visited Ocean Beach
There were kids his age looking at the Sea

;

not that
beauty a black stripe
long hair, come back, not even that
but now I had
a key in hand
sunny day, purple highway
both are true, believing in the end
he is waters, snow, went to hell came back blank
saw the fire, saw the ash
let it down, fell out
for the soil

weeds the world of pines
pines in their place / places
blue flags in the shrubbery, like blue flags in the woods
a wet computer in a bag of rice, and the dead one came through
    the door

;

the video was
an almost lifeless seed
and then bulbs, roots, shoots,
what tends to be shut out
from the top half of the world

;

man with zinc on his mask shape
sitting on a white Rambler in the new world
baby foot against my thigh on the J
White glasses in winter
White shades in winter, warm December
Black pieces with white / black shades underground
Lifted blue
Blue shirts on the lap
Folding smalls with words on them, folding large ones, turning
    the sleeves back

;

hands grimed in customer cash

the sky floats
like air conditioning
the dead live

the dead breathe
the sun sets

the filth I had traversed
the dirt the clan weighed down
with thought, which stuck

delivered

trampled

sank along

blank curtain to the floor, sand at the neck, he was a thing so
    long ago was more than that he slept, far apart
stairs carved out of dirt
camera obscura, the waves so cloudy
a pewter plate, coated with a layer of asphalt, it was something I read
middle of the country, my ghost cloud around
buoy hanging in the bathroom, he's in the flower,

there is no substitute

The areas of the asphalt exposed to light hardened.
The unexposed parts were washed out with lavender oil and turpentine.

Many knights have left their lives here, I shall soon have made an end of
you too,

Many knights have left their lives here, I shall soon have made
an end of you too,

my ghost cloud around
dances by the train
my death game

I waver
and fade
if you close

The door
The night could last forever
Leave the sun

Shine out
and drink a toast
To never

;

Fortune

;

fortunate

;

I took a walk with the palm trees
As the daylight fell

Ta a a a allk in to myself

Ohhhhhhhhh.

death runs clear
like blood like of that ghost

who lives
it's not an error

a dangerous fourth page
a bright slope of yellow
over a good face

a dancer dragging
a partner flat
her sweat is real
across it slowly but she wont get through
the people's furniture

;

my ghost cloud around
the union office downtown
brown hair black leather chair rose in a cup ice breakers gum
    rainbows on the shirts pinned to the wall, a tack at the neck,
tacks at each corner and shoulder
D
E
Fishermen sorting skeletal crabs, they're alive, no haunted eyes
They have no soul his death is spreading the photo
Mexico, Namibia, a molded carcass of a ship named Eduard,
    wrecked at Conception Bay in 1907, it's moving along

An isolated rural community, it's alive

An ox carved out of soft wood, it's so beautiful it only looks like
    an animal

A chest of drawers, there is life–alivliving

A chest with legs and flowers, a dark green chest

Sand in a bedroom,

Double doors, a table and its matching bench

Mud / snow in them, blood

A relief with lions and pomegranates, a dark natural finish

Three women looking down, heavy gathered cloths hanging
    behind them like animals

FASCINATE YOUR EMOTIONS!

it says in the same language

where my brother is dead

and my sister is walking

over a row of strange all-color rings in New York

Thank you Juan Amaya, Dan Bevacqua, Hannah Brooks-Motl, Shannon Burns, Francesca Chabrier, Michele Christle, Susan Cofer, Arda Collins, Stella Corso, Timothy Donnelly, Ben Estes, Brian Foley, A.F. Fowler, Peter Gizzi, Jane Gregory, James Haug, Brian Henry, Guy Hunt, Laura Hunt, Stuart Hunt, Kevin Killian, Seth Landman, Sara Majka, Lina Makdisi, Buffy Morgan, Amanda Nadelberg, JoAnna Novak, Jacob Otting, Ted Powers, Mimi Seydel, John (Grandaddy) Seydel, all of the Seydel family, James Tate, Emily Toder, Jono Tosch, Chris Ward, and Dara Wier.

Special thanks to Ben Estes & Alan Felsenthal for their valuable insights.

"Blue Takes Over" was inspired by a poem by Rachel B. Glaser. "Paradise Lost" was written by John Milton.

Grateful acknowledgement to the editors of the following journals, in which versions of some of these poems appear: *Sea Ranch, The Volta, Diagram, The Iowa Review, Everyday Genius, Tammy, BafterC, Shampoo, Conduit, Sixth Finch, and Softspot.* Thanks to *Floating Wolf Quarterly* for publishing several of these poems as a chapbook titled *New Clouds.*

OTHER TITLES FROM THE SONG CAVE: